Royal Babies

A CELEBRATION
THROUGH HISTORY

Royal Babies

A CELEBRATION THROUGH HISTORY

Annie Bullen & Gill Knappett

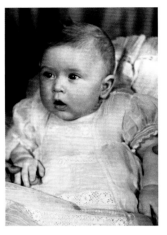
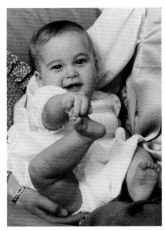

Front cover: The Duchess of Cambridge cradles her newborn son outside the Lindo Wing at St Mary's Hospital in London in April 2018.

Inside front cover: Baby Princess Elizabeth with her mother, then the Duchess of York, in 1926.

Title page: Queen Victoria with her daughter Princess Beatrice, granddaughter Princess Victoria of Hesse and great-granddaughter Princess Alice (mother of the Duke of Edinburgh), *c*.1886.

Above left to right: Queen Elizabeth II, Prince Charles, Prince William and Prince George as babies.

Inside back cover: Prince William on his second birthday in 1984.

Back cover: The Royal Family at Prince Charles' christening in 1948. Looking on are (left to right): King George VI, Princess Elizabeth, the Queen Mother and (standing) the Duke of Edinburgh.

Publication in this form © Pitkin Publishing; this edition 2018.
Text copyright Pitkin Publishing.

Original text by Annie Bullen, revised by Gill Knappett.
The moral right of the authors has been asserted.

Edited by Gill Knappett and Claire Handy.
Picture research by Gill Knappett and Sophie Nickelson.
Designed by Lee-May Lim.

All images by kind permission of Press Association Images, except for: Alamy: p18, 53; Bridgeman Art Library: pp7 right, 8 left, 9 right, 10 left; Mary Evans Picture Library: inside front cover, pp6, 7 left, 9 left, 12 right, 13, 14, 21 right; The National Archives: p11

A CIP catalogue for this book is available from the British Library.
Published by Pitkin Publishing, Pavilion Books, 43 Great Ormond Street, London WC1N 3HZ
www.pavilionbooks.com

Printed in Turkey.
ISBN 978-1-84165-810-0   1/18

Contents

Royal Babies of the Past

Until recent years, royal babies were nearly always born at home, in a palace. Some eyebrows may have been raised when Princess Anne and, later, The Prince and Princess of Wales chose to break with this royal tradition, but it has now become the norm and is therefore no surprise that all three of the Duke and Duchess of Cambridge's children have been born in hospital.

In Tudor times, however, strict rules and rituals applied to royal ladies about to give birth. The confinement of a queen was literally that: she was sent into seclusion in a suite of rooms that included a Great Chamber, a birthing chamber and an oratory with a font, so that an ailing newborn could receive immediate baptism.

Anne Boleyn, pregnant with what royal astrologers confidently predicted was her husband, King Henry VIII's, longed-for male heir, took to her chamber on 26 August 1533. Before her formal entrance, she had attended Mass and invited members of the Court to a banquet in her Great Chamber. Afterwards, all male members of the court, the household, and even the King himself, were excluded from these rooms, the women within taking over traditional male duties such as pantry men and butlers. Anne, escorted by high-born ladies, was taken to her bedchamber, which, following the rules laid down, was oppressively dark and stuffy. Tapestries showing the story of St Ursula covered walls, the ceiling and even the windows. A thick carpet was laid, and keyholes and any aperture that let in the tiniest glow of light were covered. The great bed, with a wool-stuffed mattress, fine linen sheets and large pillows filled with downy feathers, was ready for her. Alongside it were two cradles: one the formal state cradle, upholstered in red and gold, and with a crimson and ermine

Right: Greenwich Palace, named Palace of Placentia ('Pleasant Place') by King Henry VIII who was born there in 1491. His daughter Elizabeth, later Queen Elizabeth I, was also born there in 1533. The palace was demolished in 1694.

A View of the ANCIENT ROYAL PALACE, call'd, PLACENTIA, in East Greenwich.
Copied from an Engraving, published by the Society of Antiquaries of London.

counterpane to match that on the Queen's bed; and another 'cradle of tree' made of carved wood, painted gold. Braziers had been lit and open bottles of scent perfumed the air, making the room hot and airless.

The rules for the birth of a royal child dictated that the confinement should begin four to six weeks before the expected date of delivery. Anne, probably pregnant before her wedding on 25 January 1533, went into labour on 7 September, giving birth to a healthy baby girl. The official story was that the baby was premature.

That baby, who was welcomed by her father despite his longing for a son, eventually became the long-reigning Queen Elizabeth I. She was, of course, known as the 'Virgin Queen' (although that status has been questioned by some historians) and bore no children, so never had to face the claustrophobia of the royal bedchamber.

The protocol for royal birth had been exercised for centuries but these 'rules' for the confinement, followed by Anne Boleyn and other queens and royal ladies, were refined by another royal mother in 1485. Lady Margaret Beaufort, married at the age of 12 to Edmund Tudor in November 1455, was only 13 when he died just a year later. She was pregnant and gave birth to her son, Henry, at Pembroke Castle on 28 January 1457. Henry was later to defeat Richard III at the Battle of Bosworth Field on 22 August 1485, becoming Henry VII, the first Tudor King of England. Lady Margaret, who promoted and founded educational establishments (including St John's College, Cambridge, founded by her estate), detailed in writing the conditions that should be followed for all royal births.

Above left: King Henry VIII with his son, Edward, and his daughters, Mary and Elizabeth. The figure seen in the background is their jester, Will Sommers.

Above right: A portrait of the young Princess Elizabeth (later Queen Elizabeth I) painted by Robert Peake the Elder in 1603.

Above: A 1694 oil painting of James II and his family by Pierre Mignard. James and his second wife, Mary of Modena, are shown with their children. At the time of his birth, their son, James Stuart, later James III, was subject to claims that he was smuggled into the Queen's bed in a warming pan.

In 1688 a son was born to the Catholic King James II and his second wife, Mary of Modena. British people had tolerated James' Catholic government because he had no heir to perpetuate it. But when Mary's pregnancy was announced, there was consternation and rumours spread that the Queen was not pregnant, and that another woman's baby would be smuggled into the birthchamber. So Mary had to endure giving birth with a room full of witnesses – accounts vary between 76 and 200. Despite this invasion of the mother's privacy, rumours persisted that the baby was not hers but was brought by sleight-of-hand into her bed by means of a warming pan. Thus began the tradition, that most royal mothers could not avoid, of the birth being verified by a minister of the Crown. This custom, to prove legitimacy, was observed until well into the 20th century, although by then, the minister waited in an adjoining room. When she was expecting the future Edward VII in 1841, Queen Victoria decided that only one Cabinet minister would be required, and from then on, the Home Secretary was asked to attend. The last occasion when the Home Secretary was called upon to carry out this delicate duty was at the birth of Princess Alexandra of Kent in 1936.

Royal children of the past have often been brought up separated for long periods from their parents. Political situations might mean exile, while the very real fear of plague in the cities gave rise to the setting up of households in the country where the children were sent with their wet-nurses and a bevy of servants to look after them. In charge was a high-born lady or governess who would oversee the household. 'Rockers' were employed to keep the royal cradle on the move, while the wet-nurse, preferably one who was healthy looking and

rosy cheeked, was an important member of the household. She was important enough to the baby's wellbeing to have another servant taste her food – just in case someone tried to slip in poison that would affect her royal charge. These separate households were expensive to maintain with their yeomen, grooms, a chaplain, a clerk, minstrels and flute players, acrobats, a laundress and wood-bearers, among others.

Royal children born in later centuries had a safer, if much more dull, time. On 24 May 1819 the child christened Alexandrina Victoria, HRH Princess Victoria of Kent was born. Her father, Edward, Duke of Kent, died eight months later and her grandfather, George III, just six days after his son. Victoria was an only child and her mother, the overbearing Marie Louise Victoria, Duchess of Kent, employed a food-taster just in case her daughter was threatened.

Princess Victoria was brought up in the family apartments at Kensington Palace, forbidden to mix with other children and with little chance of seeing much of the outside world. She was in turn spoiled and punished by her mother and governess. When she was good, she was allowed to ride her white donkey in Kensington Gardens, led by a groom using blue ribbons. With her hair in its carefully constructed corkscrew curls, she would eat breakfast, attended by her page, on the palace lawns in summer. She was under constant surveillance from over-protective adults – never allowed to be alone in a room with a servant (unless a governess or nurse), never allowed to walk downstairs without holding someone's hand and always sleeping in the same room as her mother. When she had a tantrum – and she often did – she was locked in her room as a punishment.

Above left: A miniature showing the young Princess Victoria with her mother, the Duchess of Kent.

Above right: Princess Victoria, later Queen Victoria; an 1830 portrait in oils by Richard Westall.

The sad deaths of two royal babies left the way clear for Queen Victoria, later known as 'the grandmother of Europe', to become Queen in 1837. Although she was the granddaughter of King George III, her three uncles and her father all came before her in the royal line. Her two eldest uncles, the Prince Regent (later King George IV) and Frederick, Duke of York, had no children; her other uncle, the Duke of Clarence, not only managed to produce ten illegitimate children with actress Dorothea Jordan, but also, later, two baby girls with his wife – one born in 1819, the same year as Victoria. But both the infants, who took precedence over Victoria in the line of succession, died soon after birth. After George III's death in 1820, Victoria's uncle, the Prince Regent, became King George IV, and the next brother, the Duke of York, died in 1827. The Duke of Clarence inherited the throne, as King William IV in 1830 and, on his death in 1837, Victoria, just 18, became Queen.

Her marriage to her cousin, Prince Albert, was a love match and they went on, famously, to have nine children. The eldest, also named Victoria, was born on 21 November 1840. It is said that Queen Victoria did not enjoy pregnancy, thought breastfeeding a disgusting practice and viewed newborn babies as ugly little creatures. However, she enjoyed their antics as toddlers and spent a lot of time at her much-loved Osborne House, on the Isle of Wight, sketching them as they played. But as they grew and developed individual personalities, she found them hard to understand and cope with. Especially difficult, to her mind, was the behaviour of her oldest son and heir, Albert (Bertie) Edward. His personality

Below: A painting by Sir Edwin Landseer of Queen Victoria and Prince Albert's eldest child, the Princess Royal, Victoria, born in 1840. Shown with the baby is Prince Albert's favourite greyhound, Eos.

matched her own and she dealt with his sulks and fits of temper which so upset her by keeping him on a very tight rein – as her mother had with her. When Prince Albert died in 1861, Victoria blamed his premature passing, in part, on her son's scandalous liaison with an actress, which had upset his father considerably.

When Bertie, Prince of Wales, eventually succeeded in 1901, he was almost 60 and had been married to the outgoing Princess Alexandra of Denmark for 38 years. Alexandra loved her babies – and dreaded Queen Victoria's interference in their upbringing. Each of her six children was, apparently, born prematurely. This frustrated her mother-in-law who wanted to be present and give advice at their births. One biographer suggests that the canny Alexandra deliberately gave Victoria the wrong delivery dates so that she could avoid the unwelcome presence in the birthing chamber.

Alexandra was the first royal mother to show what we would regard today as modern care for her children. She was devoted to each of them and loved to race up to their nursery, donning an apron, to bathe them herself and, with goodnight kisses, tuck them up in bed. She was able to give so much of herself to their care because by the time her husband became King, her surviving children were grown-up. Sadly, her eldest son, Prince Albert Victor, had died of influenza at the age of 28 in 1892; her youngest child, Prince Alexander John, died at just one day old in 1871.

Alexandra's second son, Prince George, born in 1865, married Princess Mary of Teck, who had been the fiancée of George's brother, Prince Albert. George ascended the throne after the death of his father, Edward VII, in 1910 and was crowned King George V. It was he who became grandfather to the child who would, one day, become Queen Elizabeth II.

Above: Queen Victoria and Prince Albert had nine children, the first born in 1840 and the last in 1857.

A Royal Destiny

The year was 1921, and Britain was still recovering from the effects of the First World War. Young Prince Albert, the second son of King George V, shyly asked the pretty daughter of the Earl of Strathmore to be his wife. But the young woman, Lady Elizabeth Bowes-Lyon, turned him down.

'Bertie' was not to be deterred and asked her again the following year, when she was a bridesmaid to his sister, Princess Mary. But again he was disappointed. Despite his shyness, he did not give up. The following year, his persistence paid off and the couple, the Duke and Duchess of York, were married in Westminster Abbey on 26 April 1923.

Bertie's father, the 'Sailor King' who had steered his people through the four years of wartime austerity, had changed the Royal Family's name in 1917 from Saxe-Coburg-Gotha to Windsor, showing his commitment to a fully British way of life.

George V had never expected to become king, but when his older brother, Prince Albert, died in 1892, his naval career was brought to an abrupt end. He assumed the duties of heir to the throne, and he and his wife raised their family of five sons and a daughter at York Cottage on the Sandringham Estate in Norfolk. There was rejoicing on the arrival of their first child in 1894. The boy, whom they named Edward, was regarded by the nation as the future king and became heir presumptive when his grandfather, Edward VII, died in 1910 and his father ascended the throne.

As Edward, Prince of Wales, grew to manhood, his life became dissimilar to that of his younger brother, who, by the age of 28, was a happily married family man. Edward developed a reputation as a dilettante and a playboy – and he showed no signs of settling

Right: Prince Albert, later George VI, aged 18, during his service in the Royal Navy.

Far right: Lady Elizabeth Bowes-Lyon, aged seven, in 1907. She was to become Queen Elizabeth in 1937 and, later, the Queen Mother.

down. Bertie, who had served with both the Royal Navy and the newly formed Royal Air Force – becoming, in 1919, the first member of the Royal Family to qualify as a pilot – lived life very differently. After his marriage, Bertie settled comfortably into life with his young wife at their home at 145 Piccadilly, undertaking royal duties with her, including a tour of Kenya and Uganda in 1924 and 1925. Although he suffered a lack of self-confidence and a dread of public speaking because of a persistent stammer, the support of his wife and services of a speech therapist, Lionel Logue, eased his anxiety. His wife, the ninth of ten children of an energetic and loving family, helped him to enjoy life and to value a comfortable domestic situation.

And when, towards the end of 1925, they knew they were expecting their first child, due in the spring of 1926, their happiness was unbounded. They foresaw a close and happy family life, untroubled by heavy responsibility.

Although King George V was a second son and not born to rule, he had 18 years to prepare for kingship following the unexpected death of his elder brother in 1892. His own son, Prince Albert, Duke of York, was not so lucky. Dreading the public spotlight, and cherishing a peaceful and private home life, his world changed within a few days when his older brother, King Edward VIII, abdicated in December 1936 after ruling for only 11 months. Prince Albert, second in line to the throne, would become King.

Above: Lady Elizabeth Bowes-Lyon with her family at Glamis Castle in 1923. Seated (from left): Lady Elizabeth Bowes-Lyon, Miss Betty Cator, Miss Betty Malcolm, Lady Strathmore, Lady Elphinstone, Lady Glamis. Sitting on the ground is Cecilia Bowes-Lyon, the daughter of Lord and Lady Glamis. Standing are: Lord Elphinstone, Lord Glamis, Lord Strathmore, Captain Malcolm and the Hon. James Stuart.

Princess Elizabeth

There was much joy in the Royal Family when, on 21 April 1926, a baby daughter was born to the Duke and Duchess of York in London. The news was of great interest to the British people, but there was no expectation that this baby would, one day, become Queen, although she was third in the line of succession to the throne. There seemed no reason why her 'Uncle David', the Prince of Wales, the King's eldest son, should not succeed his father in due course.

Her parents, Elizabeth and Bertie, were living, temporarily, at 17 Bruton Street, Mayfair, a house that belonged to the grandfather of the Duchess, who chose to have her baby at home. Princess Elizabeth was born, by Caesarean section, at 2.40am. Bulletins reassured the public that mother and baby were both doing well.

'We always wanted a child to make our happiness complete,' the Duke, delighted by the arrival of his daughter, wrote to his mother, Queen Mary. Her Majesty was clearly happy too, recording in her diary: 'Such a relief and joy,' adding that the new baby was 'a little darling with lovely complexion and pretty fair hair.'

Baby Elizabeth was not short of exquisite clothes, handmade from first-rate materials. The newspapers reported that her grandmothers, the Queen of England and Lady Strathmore, together with her mother, the Duchess of York, had personally stitched the Princess's layette, assisted by the inmates of charitable institutions, often 'poor gentlewomen', who helped to make the fine lawn and muslin frocks, and little bonnets and jackets.

Below: Princess Elizabeth of York in her cradle in 1926.

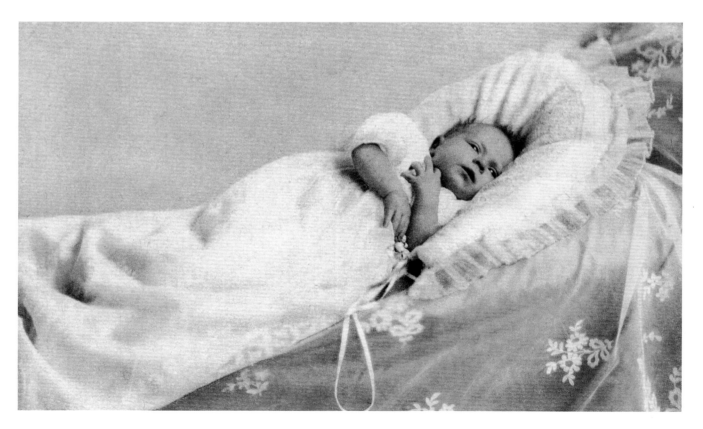

The first grandchild of King George V was named Elizabeth Alexandra Mary – for her mother (Queen Elizabeth), the King's mother (Queen Alexandra), who had died six months earlier, and for her paternal grandmother (Queen Mary).

Princess Elizabeth's upbringing, in a close-knit family atmosphere, was very different from that of her father, whose relationship with his own exacting father was often remote and difficult. But the infant Elizabeth charmed the King, who doted on his beautiful baby granddaughter, paying her the attention he had never given to his own children. She, in turn, loved to chat and play with 'Grandpa England' and her grandmother, Queen Mary.

Perhaps it was less of a surprise that Elizabeth also enjoyed her days with her maternal grandparents – having raised ten children of their own and with several grandchildren already, there was not much that the Princess's mother's parents did not know about entertaining young children.

Although the Duchess of York was as much a 'hands-on' mother as her circumstances and duties permitted, the baby Elizabeth had excellent care from her nanny, Clara Knight, known as 'Alla', who looked after her young charge from the earliest days.

Princess Elizabeth's christening ceremony, on 29 May, a few weeks after her birth, was held in the private chapel at Buckingham Palace and conducted by the Anglican Archbishop of York, Cosmo Gordon Lang, who baptised her in the traditional Lily Font with water from the river Jordan. Her godparents were King George V and Queen Mary (her paternal grandparents), Claude Bowes-Lyon (her maternal grandfather), Prince Arthur, Duke of Connaught (her father's great-uncle), Princess Mary (her paternal aunt) and Lady Elphinstone (her maternal aunt).

Above: Princess Elizabeth is christened at Buckingham Palace in May 1926. Seated in the front are (left to right): Lady Elphinstone (elder sister to the Duchess of York), Queen Mary, the Duchess of York with her daughter, Princess Elizabeth, the Countess of Strathmore and Princess Mary (sister of the Duke of York). Standing (left to right) are: the Duke of Connaught, King George V, the Duke of York and the Earl of Strathmore.

Above: Outside her home at 145 Piccadilly: two-year-old Princess Elizabeth with her nanny, Clara Knight, in 1928.

The year following the birth of baby Elizabeth was a difficult one for her parents. The Duke and Duchess of York had been invited by the Australians to open the new Parliament House in Canberra. They would also promote trade between Britain and Australia, so the six-month tour was of economic as well as diplomatic importance. They were to travel by sea on HMS *Renown*, and there was no question of their adored first-born leaving the comforts of home for such a length of time. Before and during the trip, the Duchess, especially, fretted at leaving her child behind: 'Feel very miserable at leaving the baby,' she wrote in her diary. 'Went up & played with her & she was so sweet.'

The Duchess knew that the child would be well cared for by the ever-vigilant Alla and by her grandparents, but she also knew she would miss so many stages of her baby's life, not least her first birthday. The King and Queen were sent regular accounts of Elizabeth's progress, including how she waved goodbye, saying 'ta-ta' and 'by-eee'. Photographs of the tiny Princess were also received, including one that showed a laughing baby; a note attached, written by the nanny, Clara Knight, read: 'If Mummy looks into my wide open mouth with a little magnifying glass, she will see my two teeth.'

When, at last, the royal parents arrived home, their first thoughts were of their daughter, now a toddler. They moved with her to their new home, 145 Piccadilly, whose windows faced those of Buckingham Palace. When Elizabeth grew a little older, she was given a small telescope which she could use to 'spy' on her grandfather the King who, in turn, would train his telescope from Buckingham Palace on her, so that they could wave at each other. It was not unknown for the King to visit his son and daughter-in-law and, with no thought for royal dignity, get down on all fours so that Elizabeth could climb on his back for a ride around the room, something he would not have dreamed of doing with his own children. When the toddler was two, he became seriously ill and spent some time recuperating at Bognor Regis – with plenty of visits from his little granddaughter. Even stern Queen Mary unbent enough to enjoy time on the beach with her, making sandcastles.

Elizabeth's mother – brought up in a large family, enjoying country pursuits, games, outings and the support of several brothers and sisters – wanted to give her own child the same happy childhood. Weekends were spent at Royal Lodge, Windsor, and soon the little girl received a present that was to induce a lifelong passion: Peggy, a fat Shetland pony, was hers to love, look after and ride at Windsor. The Princess had already caught the family obsession with dogs but her love of horses and the freedom they have brought her started in her very early childhood when Peggy, the first of many ponies, became a part of the royal household.

Below: A young Princess Elizabeth playing with her doll's pram in the grounds of Royal Lodge, Windsor Great Park.

Princess Margaret

Although the month was August, the night was cold and the weather unseasonal. Thunder echoed and rolled around the hills, while frequent flashes of lightning lit up the sandstone walls and fairy-tale turrets of rain-lashed Glamis Castle, the ancient family seat of the Scottish earls of Strathmore and Kinghorne in the County of Angus.

Despite the pouring rain and the storm raging overhead, villagers, wrapped up against the elements, waited by the north gate of the castle for news of a royal birth – the first in direct line of succession to the throne in Scotland for more than 300 years. The Duchess of York, daughter-in-law to King George V and youngest daughter of the 14th Earl of Strathmore, had chosen to travel to her family home to give birth to her second baby. At 9.22pm on 21 August 1930, a 6lb 11oz girl, a second granddaughter to the King and herself fourth in line to the British throne, was born. Named Margaret Rose, she was said to be as pretty as a picture, with large blue eyes and a clear pink and white complexion.

Soon mother and baby travelled back to London to their home, just across Green Park from Buckingham Palace. As Margaret grew, she shared the same childhood delights and passions as her older sister 'Lilibet' (a family name coined by a very young Margaret, unable to pronounce 'Elizabeth'). They both enjoyed the countryside and riding, romping with their favourite corgis and picnicking outside, whether at Royal Lodge, Windsor, their weekend residence, or at Balmoral, the Royal Family's Scottish estate where the whole family then, as now, gathered for summer holidays.

In London, the children could gaze from their windows at the front of their home across to the grand palace where 'Grandpa England' lived with their grandmother, Queen Mary, while their garden backed on to Hyde Park, and many Londoners went out of their way to stroll past the railings to see the two little Princesses at play.

Below: Glamis Castle, the Queen Mother's family home, where Princess Margaret was born in 1930.

Right: Princess Margaret Rose, aged three, toddles in front of her nannies in 1933.

Below right: Sisters Princess Margaret and Princess Elizabeth in 1933.

While Elizabeth had a serious, thoughtful streak, it was said that her little sister was full of fun and often mischievous. Family history records an occasion when the girls, accompanied by their grandmother and mother, were taken to see the work of disabled ex-servicemen. The younger Princess spent some time examining a wheelchair, working out how to ring its bell – which she did with some vigour before anyone could stop her.

Despite their different natures, the two sisters were inseparable during early childhood. Both loved outdoor activities, but while the quieter, less demonstrative Elizabeth was pony-mad, Margaret enjoyed play-acting and music, dancing and singing with noticeable ability from early childhood. She was also a talented mimic, which on occasion somewhat startled certain members of the royal circle. Elizabeth observed her younger sister drawing all the attention and did not mind one bit. She is said to have remarked to her governess: 'It's so much easier when Margaret's there – everyone laughs at what Margaret says.'

They shared their nanny, Alla, and, as soon as they were old enough for lessons, were taught by their mother and their governess, Marion Crawford, who stayed with them for 16 years.

Princess Margaret and her older sister were noted for their gentleness and beautiful manners; while their father took pleasure in his older child's intelligence and quiet self-possession, he doted on his younger daughter's joyful, outgoing nature. He described Elizabeth as 'my pride' while Margaret was always 'my joy'.

Prince Philip

When the young Princesses Elizabeth and Margaret began their history lessons, they knew little of their distant cousin Prince Philip of Greece, though, like the sisters, he was a great-great-grandchild of the redoubtable Queen Victoria, who had died in 1901. However, the early childhood of the three young royals could not have been more different.

Elizabeth and Margaret, as the beloved grandchildren of the King of England, lived in comfort in a close and caring family. Their baby days and early childhood were ruled by the nursery routine dictated by their nanny and governess, which gave a sense of security.

Philip was born on 10 June 1921 at his parents' villa, 'Mon Repos', on the sunny island of Corfu. His soldier father, Prince Andrea (Andrew) of Greece, was commanding the Greek army's 12th division in Asia Minor and did not see his son for the first three months of his life.

The young Prince came into the world during a time of turmoil in the Balkan nations. His mother, Princess Alice, and his four older sisters lived in the house left to them by his paternal grandfather, George I of Greece, who had been assassinated in March 1913. Philip's uncle, Constantine I, who ruled Greece during the first Balkan War, suffered exile, as did Philip's father, Andrea. Another uncle, Alexander, who briefly took the Crown during Constantine's exile, died of blood poisoning. His Russian relations, the Romanovs – including his great aunts on his mother's side, the Empress Alix and Princess Elisabeth, and his father's cousin Tsar Nicholas II and his family – had been murdered by Lenin's Red Army in 1918. Philip was

Below left: Prince Andrea (Andrew) of Greece and Princess Alice of Battenberg, Prince Philip's parents, married at Darmstadt, near Frankfurt in Germany, October 1903.

Below right: Prince Philip at the age of 14 months.

barely a year old when his father narrowly escaped being sentenced to death by the new Republican Greek government. He and his family fled from their villa in Corfu into exile.

Andrea and Alice had married in 1903 after a short engagement. The wedding, at Alice's family home, Darmstadt, just south of Frankfurt, was a magnificent affair, lasting two days. The couple lived in Athens where they had four daughters, despite the often unsettling political climate as the Balkan Wars put pressure on the military and on the King and his family.

This pressure meant that the Greek royal family, including Andrea and Alice and their four daughters, were in exile in Switzerland in the months before Philip's birth in 1921. Suddenly the Greeks voted to restore the monarchy and they returned – Alice expecting her fifth and last baby. While Andrea, now a major-general in the Greek army, returned to his military duties in Athens, Alice and the children travelled across the sea to their villa on Corfu, where the family were helped by an English housekeeper, a handyman and Alice's elderly nanny, Miss Emily Roose. 'Mon Repos' had no modern comforts such as electricity or running hot water, but it was secluded and in a beautiful position, looking over the Ionian Sea.

Above: Prince Philip, aged two, with his mother, Princess Alice, in 1924. The family were living in exile in a Paris suburb at this time.

Contact with Andrea became difficult when, on 9 June, he was given command of a division, leaving Athens for Smyrna, to lead troops in the on-going Turkish campaign. Early on the morning of the following day, Alice, now 36 years old, went into labour and was helped onto the villa's dining-room table by the local doctor who decided this was the best place for her to give birth. A baby boy, later registered as Philippos, was delivered at 10am. The child was sixth in line to the Greek throne.

Alice wrote to her family at Darmstadt that her new baby was 'a splendid healthy child'. She confirmed that she had had an easy delivery and was enjoying the pleasant sea-air from her chaise longue on the terrace. The blonde-haired, blue-eyed Philip, the longed-for son, was the darling of a household full of women. He was a chubby, happy baby, fussed over by his adoring mother and four older sisters.

When Philip was three months old, Alice's father, Louis, Marquis of Milford Haven, died. She travelled with her infant son to Osborne House, on the Isle of Wight, for the burial. There the smiling baby was passed around an assortment of aunts and uncles for kisses and cuddles and general admiration. On their return to Corfu, Alice was surprised and delighted to find Andrea home on leave; he was thrilled to hold his baby son in his arms for the first time.

Although Prince Philip was, briefly, sixth in line to the Greek throne, he has no Greek blood. His great-grandfather was King Christian IX of Denmark whose son, Prince William, Philip's grandfather, was sent to Greece at the tender age of 17 to be crowned their king. King George I of Greece, as he became, had eight children, one of whom, Andrea, was Prince Philip's father.

Philip's mother, Alice, was Queen Victoria's great-granddaughter. Her mother, Princess Victoria, married Prince Louis of Battenberg, who eventually became First Sea Lord and 1st Marquis of Milford Haven. Alice, despite being born deaf, was noted for her beauty, poise and cleverness. Her younger brother, Louis, became Admiral of the Fleet, Earl Mountbatten of Burma.

Prince Philip's father met his mother in 1902 when both were guests at the coronation of King Edward VII, which had been delayed because of the King's sudden appendicitis. The young couple fell in love and became engaged.

Philip was almost a year old, and already standing up, when his maternal grandmother, the newly widowed Victoria, and Alice's sister, Louise, came to stay. The doting grandmother and aunt were delighted with the happy little boy. Louise wrote that he laughed all day and that she had never seen such a cheerful baby.

But not long afterwards the family had to flee for their lives. The Greek army was beaten in the Turkish campaign, the country humiliated and Andrea's brother, King Constantine, abdicated and fled into exile. Philip's father was banished from Greece for life. The family slipped quietly out of Greece on the British cruiser *Calypso*. At the Corfu villa, Philip's sisters hastily packed essential possessions, and burned letters, papers and documents before embarking for their new life in exile. Philip, just 18 months old, remembered nothing of the escape, when he slept on board in a crib made from a roughly converted fruit crate.

They settled, eventually, in Paris where they lived at St Cloud, but by the time Philip was nine, his mother had become ill and was taken to a Swiss psychiatric sanatorium. Philip had already been sent to Cheam, an English preparatory school; his father moved to a small flat in Monte Carlo; his sisters married and moved away. After completing his secondary education at Gordonstoun in Scotland, he chose a naval career, training at the Royal Naval College, Dartmouth, where, in July 1939, he was to meet his 13-year-old cousin, Princess Elizabeth – a meeting that was to change the course of his life.

Left: Seven-year-old Prince Philip (left) rides on the sands at Constanza in 1928 with his cousin Michael who was King of Romania.

Prince Charles

When Princess Elizabeth and Prince Philip made their first official overseas visit as a couple to France in the baking hot days of May 1948, no one guessed that the glamorous young woman, who charmed the French public and dignitaries alike, might have been feeling unwell. The couple, married just six months earlier, were expecting their first child. But Elizabeth coped perfectly, keeping her happy news secret.

The Duke and Duchess of Edinburgh were still waiting for their first real home. Clarence House, next to St James's Palace in London, was being refurbished for them and they were living in a rented property near Windsor. They moved back into Buckingham Palace, where the ornate Buhl Room was converted into a delivery suite for the arrival of the baby who would be second in line of succession to the throne. Previously, royal babies were born at home with top doctors and nurses in attendance. This tradition for an heir to the throne was broken only when Prince Charles' son, Prince William, was born in hospital – albeit in a private wing.

On the early evening of 14 November 1948, Philip – never the most patient of men – was dividing his time between swimming in the palace pool and playing squash with his equerry, Mike Parker. Elizabeth had gone into labour 24 hours earlier; she was attended by doctor Sir William Gilliatt and nursing sister Helen Rowe, so Philip knew she was in good hands and physical activity was the way he coped with the long, tense wait.

Suddenly King George VI's private secretary 'Tommy' Lascelles appeared at the door of the squash court. The news was good, and Philip raced upstairs, grabbing the roses, carnations and a bottle of champagne ordered earlier. As Elizabeth, sleepy from medication, opened her eyes, he handed her the flowers and kissed her as he gazed at their baby son who was in a cot by her side.

'Her Royal Highness the Princess Elizabeth, Duchess of Edinburgh, was safely delivered of a Prince at 9.14 o'clock this evening. Her Royal Highness and the infant Prince are both doing well'

Right: Princess Elizabeth was expecting her first child when she attended the Bath and West and Southern Counties Show at Cardiff in May 1948.

Far right: Prince Charles, fair-haired and blue-eyed, was almost five months old when this photograph was taken at Buckingham Palace in April 1949.

Above: Proud parents: a delighted Princess Elizabeth and Prince Philip show off their first son, Prince Charles, in 1949.

read the handwritten notice attached to the Buckingham Palace railings by the King's press secretary, raising a cheer and a rendition of 'For he's a jolly good fellow' from the 3,000 people who had gathered outside, waiting for the news.

By the evening of the following day, more than 4,000 telegrams had been received and a deluge of presents, from hand-knitted hats, bootees and matinee jackets to teddy bears, began to arrive.

But although there were photographs of the baby and bulletins about him, one thing remained a mystery: what was he to be called? Speculation deepened as the name of the next heir to the throne was not announced until his christening, a full month later.

When the news came, on 15 December, that the baby was to be called Charles Philip Arthur George, many were surprised. The name Charles had not been used by the Royal Family for more than 300 years, after the unhappy reigns of Charles I and Charles II.

Both Elizabeth and Philip enjoyed those early days of parenthood, when they were relatively free to spend time with their baby son. Prince Philip was a good and involved parent with all his children when they were little – playing with them, reading stories and teaching them to fish and enjoy outdoor pursuits.

The following year saw the family moving into Clarence House, refurbished at last. Charles was safely established in his blue and white nursery, sleeping in the cot that had belonged to his mother and aunt. The new nursery regime was overseen by nanny Helen Lightbody, an experienced Scottish nurse, whose strict manner gave her the nickname 'No-Nonsense Lightbody', and a young girl who was to become an important part of Prince Charles' life: Mabel Anderson.

Mabel, a policeman's daughter, was 22 – almost the same age as the Duchess of Edinburgh – when she replied to an advertisement for an assistant nanny, not knowing it was from the royal household. Mabel was, said Charles, 'warm, loving, sympathetic and caring'. It was Mipsy, as her young charge called her, who put Charles to bed, read him stories, taught him to say his prayers and brush his teeth. It was she he turned to when he fell and grazed his knee or felt unhappy. Both he and, later, Princess Anne, clearly loved and listened to her and she was invited to many private Royal Family gatherings over the years.

Right: The Queen Mother with Prince Charles and his sister, Princess Anne, in the grounds of Royal Lodge, Windsor Great Park, in 1954.

Right: Prince Charles and Princess Anne with their great-aunt and uncle, Earl and Countess Mounbatten, on the beach at Peters Pool during their visit to Valetta, Malta in 1954.

Princess Anne

Above: Princess Elizabeth with her children on Princess Anne's first birthday.

At precisely 3.30pm on 15 August 1950, a Royal Salute was fired in Hyde Park by the King's Troop of the Royal Horse Artillery. The gunfire welcomed the latest addition to the Royal Family, a baby girl, into the world. Prince Charles, almost two, was joined in the nursery by his sister, who was born at home, Clarence House, just before noon, weighing exactly 6lbs.

Her father, Prince Philip, brought bottles of champagne to toast her health with the staff, while her grandfather, King George VI, was tracked down on the grouse moors at Balmoral to be told the good news. The baby's grandmother, the Queen, visited twice that day to hold her newborn granddaughter.

Two weeks later the baby's name was announced: Anne Elizabeth Alice Louise, Princess Anne of Edinburgh. When the Registrar visited Clarence House to complete Princess Anne's birth certificate, he handed Prince Philip his baby daughter's identity card, a ration book and bottles of cod-liver oil and orange juice, as was the practice in those post-war years.

The nursery routine accommodated the pretty blonde curly haired child. It soon became obvious, however, that although the two children loved each other dearly and enjoyed playing together, their natures were very different. Charles, thoughtful and shy, artistic and a sensitive daydreamer, sometimes lacked confidence. His younger sister, however, was an extrovert and could be high-spirited and a little naughty. As soon as she could choose, this bright little tomboy preferred wearing dungarees or trousers to dresses. Anne loved sports and inherited her mother's passion for horses. She and brother Charles learned to ride on a roan gelding called William. Although Anne was the bolder of the two on horseback, both became accomplished riders. Anne is a horsewoman of the first order, eventually becoming a member of the British Olympic equestrian team.

But rosettes were in the future, and Anne was a lively toddler of 18 months when her grandfather, the King, died in February 1952. Life changed in an instant. Charles and Anne, children of the new monarch, had to leave the familiar surroundings of Clarence House for the overwhelmingly vast and grand Buckingham Palace, moving to the nursery floor where familiar items from Clarence House – the large Tudor doll's house, toy soldiers and cuckoo clock – were waiting for them. It was here that they received their early schooling from governess Catherine Peebles, their tutor and mentor until they started school, with Princess Anne boarding at Benenden School in Kent from the age of 13.

Princes Andrew & Edward

Ten years after the birth of Princess Anne, the nation learned that The Queen was expecting another child. Prince Andrew Albert Christian Edward was born in the grand Belgian Suite on the ground floor of Buckingham Palace's garden wing on 19 February 1960. Soon after his birth The Queen wrote to her second cousin, Lady Mary Cambridge: 'The baby is adorable, and is very good, and putting on weight well. Both the older children are completely riveted by him and all in all, he's going to be terribly spoilt by all of us, I'm sure.'

Four years later, on 10 March 1964, Prince Edward Antony Richard Louis was born in the same room, completing the family. The two boys, Andrew and Edward, were the first children to be born to a reigning monarch since their great-great-great-grandmother, Queen Victoria, gave birth to her youngest daughter, Beatrice, in 1857. Andrew, and later Edward, were looked after by the favourite royal nanny, Mabel Anderson, with the help of a newly appointed assistant, the 29-year-old June Waller.

Following royal tradition, Andrew was taught at home by a governess (and by The Queen who helped him learn to read and count) until he was eight, when he went away to school, as did his younger brother.

It seems Andrew was a mischievous young boy, being caught tying together the shoelaces of castle guards as they stood at attention – and somehow turning the swimming pool at Windsor Castle into a giant bubble bath on one memorable occasion.

Right: Prince Andrew, at seven months, holds hands with his sister, Princess Anne, and his father, the Duke of Edinburgh.

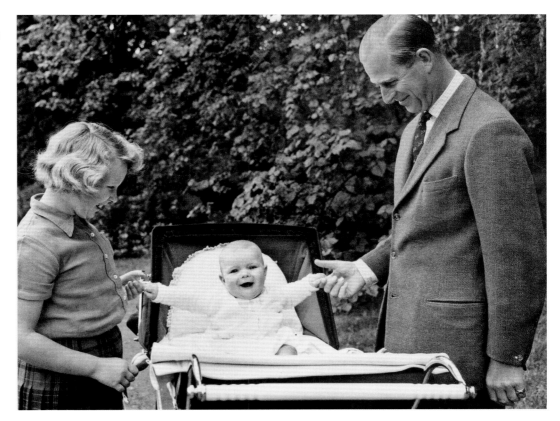

Andrew enjoyed several outings with his nursemaid, June, who wrote to a friend in March 1963: '... I took Andrew on a *bus*!! to Paddington Station to see the trains. He was thrilled to bits and couldn't see everything fast enough – we even bought sweets in a kiosk there and no one gave us a second glance, it was marvellous.' She wrote of another outing: 'We also went to the zoo about a fortnight ago – two other children and nans. It was great fun – again, no one recognised him – but then again we looked rather a disreputable lot in mackintoshes, etc! He muddled in with all the other children at the chimps' tea party and he might have belonged to anyone!'

In another letter, June described the eight-month-old Edward, calling him an 'absolute poppet' and a 'funny, cheeky little thing – not a bit like Andrew'. At that age Edward, the proud possessor of four teeth, and weighing 20lb 8oz, enjoyed propelling himself across the floor on his elbows, knees and tummy. 'London being what it is, the colour of his clothes is nobody's business,' wrote June, adding that the young Prince 'looks permanently like a scruffy, cheeky little London sparrow, except when he is clean in bed.'

Both Andrew and Edward went to the exclusive Heatherdown Preparatory School near Ascot, in Berkshire, before following in their older brother and father's footsteps to the rugged Gordonstoun school in Moray, Scotland.

Above: Queen Elizabeth II with her two youngest children, Prince Andrew and Prince Edward, in 1965.

Buckingham Palace's Belgian Suite, named for Queen Victoria's favourite uncle, King Leopold of Belgium, was converted into a delivery ward for the arrival of The Queen's two younger sons. Today the grand, three-roomed apartment is where visiting heads of state stay when they visit the British Royal Family.

Royal Grannies & Nannies

On Prince Charles' 60th birthday in November 2008, an exhibition illustrating his early life was displayed at Windsor Castle. Among the photographs on show were those of an expertly crafted green stoneware mug, with a Celtic-style initial 'M' incised in the oxidised glaze. The words 'Charles' and 'Gordonstoun' appear on the base. This treasured object was made in the school pottery studio by the 17-year-old Charles in 1965, not for a family member, but for his former nanny, Mabel Anderson, who had been a central figure for the boy as he grew up.

Royal parents have heavy demands on them and, however much they want to be 'hands-on', it has never been possible to spend as much time in the nursery as they might like. They rely on grandparents for help, but royal children have the additional support of nannies, nursery staff and sometimes a governess, all of whom tread the fine line of giving loving care to their charges without taking the place of the royal mother or father.

Below: An outing in the park with nanny for baby Princess Elizabeth in 1929.

Above: Nanny Mabel Anderson takes Prince Charles for an outing to St James's Park on his second birthday in November 1950.

Below: Prince William with nanny Barbara Barnes in 1984.

Royal sisters the Princesses Elizabeth and Margaret were dearly cherished by their grandparents, King George V and Queen Mary, whose own children were not nearly as indulged as their granddaughters. They were also loved and looked after by their nanny, Clara Knight ('Alla'), once their own mother's nanny, and, later, when Elizabeth was four, by 'Bobo', Margaret MacDonald, who became a lifelong companion, taking on the task of royal dresser when Elizabeth became Queen. Their friendship ended only when Bobo died in 1993 at the age of 89; hers is understood to be one of the few funerals ever attended by Her Majesty.

Another stalwart was Mabel Anderson ('Mipsy'), who came to care for baby Charles and, later, Princess Anne. Mipsy became a beloved friend, accompanying the family on holiday treats and spending time with The Queen and Prince Charles, who described her as 'a haven of security, the great haven'. Mabel, when retired, returned to royal service, temporarily, to help Princess Anne care for her son, Peter. Mabel was given a grace-and-favour home in an apartment at Frogmore House in Windsor Home Park. King George VI, The Queen's father, died when Charles and Anne were very young, but Queen Elizabeth the Queen Mother loved young children and was close to both of them. Charles, especially, felt comfortable with his grandmother and turned to her with his worries and problems.

Shortly before Prince Charles turned five, a room in the nursery at Buckingham Palace was converted into a classroom where he was taught by Catherine Peebles. It was not until he was eight that it was agreed he would benefit from the company of other children and started at a school in Knightsbridge – the first heir to the throne to attend school beyond palace walls.

When Prince William, son of Prince Charles and Princess Diana, was born, his mother resolved to give her children constant attention and affection. Just a few weeks after his birth, she and Charles were committed to a long tour of Australia. Diana refused to leave her baby behind. There was worldwide approval when pictures were shown of William in the arms of his nanny, Barbara Barnes, being carried from the aircraft onto Australian soil.

Barbara Barnes was succeeded by Ruth Wallace and subsequently Jessie Webb, nannies to both Prince William and Prince Harry. Consistent in the boys' lives was Olga Powell who assisted the other nannies and spent 15 years with the princes. They kept in touch with her throughout her retirement, and, when she died in 2012, William attended her funeral, also representing Harry who was on a tour of duty in Afghanistan. Olga was there for the boys when their parents divorced, but it was their last nanny, Alexandra 'Tiggy' Legge-Bourke, who helped them through the dark days following their mother's untimely death in 1997. Tiggy remains their friend to this day.

Both William and Harry turn to their grandmother, The Queen, for advice and support and, when they were pupils at Eton College, were delighted to be able to join her for afternoon tea at nearby

Left: Two royal grandmothers (Queen Elizabeth, later the Queen Mother, and Queen Mary) sit next to Princess Elizabeth who cradles baby Princess Anne after her christening in 1950. Queen Elizabeth holds Prince Charles while his grandfather and father stand in the background.

Below: The Duke of Cambridge watches his son Prince George speaking with his great-grandmother Queen Elizabeth II at Princess Charlotte's christening in 2015. Nanny Maria Teresa Turrion Borrallo is behind.

Windsor Castle. Jessie Webb came out of retirement at the age of 71 to help with William's newborn son, Prince George, on a part-time basis in 2013. In March 2014 a full-time nanny from the famous Norland College in Bath joined the royal household: Maria Borrallo. Spanish-born Ms Borrallo has remained as nanny to the Duke and Duchess ever since, and now has three children in her charge.

The Duchess of Cambridge's parents, Michael and Carole Middleton, have always been hands-on grandparents. Prince Charles also adores his grandchildren, who are reported to enjoy playing in 'Hollyrood House' – the treehouse built into a holly tree, originally for his sons, in the gardens of his home at Highgrove in Gloucestershire.

Royal Nurseries

Below left: Parisian dolls that belonged to Princess Elizabeth and Princess Margaret at the launch of the summer exhibition, Royal Childhood, at Buckingham Palace in April 2014.

Below right: A laughing Princess Elizabeth, attending a charity ball in London in 1951, accepts a toy stove for Prince Charles from Lieutenant Michael Parker, RN (left), and the Hon. Piers St Aubyn (right) in London in 1951.

Royal babies have traditionally spent their formative years in the sensible surroundings of a room or suite of rooms known as 'the nursery', a domain ruled over by a nanny or nannies, more often than not helped by a nursery nurse and other assistants.

Queen Victoria and Prince Albert created a charming nursery at Osborne House for their children where they could enjoy family time away from public view. The nursery, with its child-size dining table and chairs, remains today as it was in 1870, and can be seen on a visit to the house, now in the care of English Heritage.

Princess Elizabeth's first nursery was small, a room in the family's temporary residence at Bruton Street, furnished and decorated by her maternal grandmother, Lady Strathmore. But soon there was much more space for the infant Elizabeth and, later, her sister Margaret Rose, when the family moved to 145 Piccadilly, a London mansion where a suite of rooms on the top floor were converted to accommodate a day nursery, a night nursery and a bathroom. The rooms all opened on to a landing, with large windows overlooking Green Park. A sense of security and comfort was established with a regular routine, nursery meals and the ever-present nanny – in the small Princesses' case, the reassuring figure of Alla. There was a rocking horse and other toys, but there were also baby garments hung to dry on airing rails. While the children played or sat to eat their breakfast or lunch, nanny would sit in her rocking chair, knitting or mending clothes. After bathtime in the evening, she would tell the girls stories before bedtime.

Rocking horses have long formed an important part of the royal nursery, with Charles I the owner of the oldest one in history, which dates to *c.*1610 and is now in the V&A Museum of Childhood, Bethnal Green, London.

From early days the children were taught good manners and restraint – when Princess Elizabeth began to crawl, she was allowed only one toy at a time to play with. During summer holidays with their mother's parents at Glamis Castle, the children stayed in the ancient nursery wing that had seen their aunts and uncles grow up. Both Prince Charles and Princess Anne were cocooned in the nursery wing at Clarence House for the first years of their lives. The day nursery, with its chintz-covered armchairs, its fireplace, radiogram and desk, was like a sitting-room in a comfortable home, but there were also small tables and chairs, designed with young children in mind. The children were both still under the age of five when their grandfather died, their mother became Queen, and they moved to Buckingham Palace, where everything was on a larger scale. By the time Charles was five, part of the day nursery at the palace was converted into a school room, complete with a desk and blackboards, so that his education could begin at home with his new governess, Catherine Peebles.

It was in the Buckingham Palace nursery that the toddler Charles played with some of his best-loved toys, including wooden bricks packed into a trolley bearing the words 'Prince Charles Express', but it was at Windsor Castle that he enjoyed one of his favourite games: taking his green Sunbeam Coupe pedal car from the nursery and racing it up and down the Grand Corridor. Prince Charles' sons, William and Harry, shared a top-floor nursery at Kensington Palace, where there were bedrooms, bathrooms, playrooms, a kitchen and dining room. Nanny Olga Powell had her own small bedsit apartment next to the boys' rooms so that she could keep an eye on them at all times.

When William, Catherine and George set up home in Anmer Hall in Norfolk, it is understood that Catherine's mother, Carole Middleton, helped source fabrics and furnishings for the nursery in preparation for the arrival of her second grandchild. Gathering colour swatches and samples from interior design outlets in Chelsea, she took care not to linger on blue or pink fabrics so as not to reveal whether she knew if the new arrival would be a boy or girl. George and Charlotte's nursery at Kensington Palace includes furniture designed by Steuart Padwick, winner of a competition held by The Worshipful Company of Furniture Makers to commemorate the birth of Princess Charlotte. The Company, granted a Royal Charter in 2013, had previously presented Prince George with a specially commissioned high chair.

Above: Prince George plays on the rocking horse presented to him by Barack Obama during the US president's visit to the UK in April 2016.

Peter & Zara Phillips

Below: Three generations: Princess Anne holds her first-born, Peter Phillips, after his christening at Buckingham Palace. The Queen is clearly taken with her first grandchild.

The Queen's eldest grandchild made history when he was born during the middle of the morning on 15 November 1977. His mother, Princess Anne, was driven to St Mary's Hospital, Paddington, by her then husband, Captain Mark Phillips, in the early hours of that day. When the baby boy arrived, weighing 7lb 9oz, a 41-gun salute, the usual signal of a royal birth, was fired at the Tower of London, but the baby, whose names were not yet announced, was given no title. He was born plain Master Phillips because Princess Anne, in spite of being The Queen's daughter, possesses no hereditary title; her son became the first royal baby to be born a commoner for more than 500 years. But that did not put a dampener on the rejoicing in his paternal grandparents' village of Great Somerford in Wiltshire, where a peal of bells was rung at the church of St Peter and St Paul in celebration of the new arrival.

In 1987, Princess Anne became the seventh to receive the title Princess Royal; although it is not an hereditary title, it is generally bestowed on the eldest daughter of the monarch. Princess Anne's great-niece, Princess Charlotte of Cambridge, will likely be granted the title.

The Queen was among the first of a clutch of visitors at the private wing of the hospital and she was clearly delighted with her first grandson, whose name, Peter Mark Andrew Phillips, was later announced. When Peter eventually arrived home to Gatcombe Park in Gloucestershire, it was to the welcoming arms of his mother's nanny, Mabel Anderson, who had been persuaded to come out of retirement to look after the latest royal baby. Miss Anderson, much loved by all the Royal Family, stayed with young Peter until he went to the pre-prep department of Beaudesert Park School, Minchinhampton, within walking distance of Gatcombe, just before a baby sister was born on 15 May 1981.

Zara Anne Elizabeth and Peter grew up together with the freedom to enjoy country life. Gatcombe is situated in beautiful, unspoiled countryside, and they were born into a family whose main interest is horses. They had access to the stables of their parents, both expert riders, and ponies of their own, which they learned to master almost as soon as they could walk – and Zara ultimately followed in Princess Anne's footsteps by competing in the Olympics, winning a silver medal at London 2012.

If there was sadness at the departure of nanny Mabel Anderson, returning to a well-earned retirement, there was also fun to be had with their new nanny, Pat Moss, who would take them out, often over to their paternal grandparents' farmhouse, just 15 miles away.

Zara followed her brother to Beaudesert Park School and Port Regis Preparatory School in Dorset. In line with royal tradition, the siblings studied at Gordonstoun in Scotland, where they both excelled in sports and where Peter, who was chosen to be head boy, played rugby for the school, while Zara represented it at hockey, athletics and gymnastics.

Zara's unusual name was the inspiration of her uncle, Prince Charles. 'The baby made a rather sudden and positive arrival,' recalled Princess Anne, 'and my brother thought Zara (a Greek name meaning "bright as the dawn") was an appropriate name.'

Top: Zara and Peter Phillips and their cousin, Prince William (centre), share a joke on Buckingham Palace balcony during their grandmother's birthday parade in 1984.

Above: Two-year-old Zara Phillips rides on the shoulders of her mother, Princess Anne.

Previous page right: Peter Phillips enjoys his father's company at the Badminton Horse Trials in 1983.

Prince William

Right from the start, Prince Charles and Princess Diana were determined that their children should have as normal a childhood as possible, although they were aware that they would be unable to spirit them away from the spotlight of public interest that would be a focus from the moment of birth.

Prince William's debut was different from that of earlier royal births of children of heirs to the throne. He was born in an ordinary hospital, albeit in a private wing, the first heir not to make his entrance in one of the royal residences. This was seen by many as a sign that the young Prince was entering a changing world, far different from that occupied by his father in 1948.

Prince William Arthur Philip Louis of Wales entered the world at 9.03pm on 21 June 1982 in the Lindo Wing of St Mary's Hospital, Paddington. His father, 33-year-old Prince Charles, next in line to the throne, had been at his wife's side and is understood to be the first royal male to be present at a birth. That evening, to chants of 'We want Charlie!' from the excited throng of people outside the hospital, the new father emerged to greet them. When one well-wisher asked if the baby looked like Prince Charles, he joked, 'No, he's lucky enough not to!'

Below: Prince William's first Christmas: with his parents at Kensington Palace in 1982.

Crowds of well-wishers and the media were waiting outside St Mary's early on the morning of 23 June when Prince Charles and Princess Diana came out of the hospital and stood proudly on the steps with their newborn son, who will one day be king. The then unnamed baby, the tag still on his wrist identifying him only as 'Baby Wales', slept peacefully in his father's arms, while cameras flashed, and journalists and television crews shouted questions to the new parents. 'The birth of our son has given us both more pleasure than you can imagine,' said a delighted Charles. 'It has made me incredibly proud and somewhat amazed.' Writing to his godmother, Lady Brabourne, soon after, he said the birth of his son meant more to him than he ever could have imagined.

William's mother nicknamed her baby 'Wills' and, later, 'Wombat', two names that have stayed with him. Princess Diana, who had worked as a nursery assistant and as a nanny, loved young children and was a devoted and imaginative mother, keeping her vow to be closely involved with her children's care. She often defied royal convention in William's upbringing, choosing his first name and buying his clothes herself. Although she had a full schedule of duties, she tried to negotiate these around William's timetable. She was demonstrative with her children and William was picked up, cuddled and kissed, often in public.

Above: Prince William was crawling when his parents took him on his first trip abroad on a visit to New Zealand in 1983.

Prince William saw far more of his parents than royal babies in the past, and some might say the much-loved young William, with his cheeky, outgoing character, was, perhaps, a little too indulged by his doting mother. He was inclined to want to rule the roost and have things his own way; for a while the tabloid press nicknamed the little boy 'William the Terrible' for his sometimes public tantrums. A new nanny, the no-nonsense Ruth Wallace, joined the nursery floor at Kensington Palace to help her colleague, Olga Powell; the two nannies were given authority by Charles and Diana to discipline the spirited youngster, reminding him of the value of good manners and aiming to teach the toddler Prince how to behave on all occasions.

When it was time for Prince William to start learning, there was no governess – he was to go to nursery school like other small children. Diana was keen that he should learn to interact with other children and to understand that there was a world outside the palace. In September 1985 he started at Mrs Mynors' Nursery School, a small private establishment, chosen by his mother, in Notting Hill Gate, less than a mile from his home at Kensington Palace. As often as she could, Diana accompanied her three-year-old son to school and collected him herself. It was at the nursery school that he earned the nickname 'Basher Wills' for his sometimes boisterous behaviour. Despite everyone's efforts, the small boy's natural character shone through when, as a pageboy at the wedding of his uncle Prince Andrew to Sarah Ferguson at Westminster Abbey in 1986, he was seen fidgeting and rolling his order of service into a makeshift trumpet.

When William was four-and-a-half, his schooling moved to the next level when he started at the upmarket Wetherby Pre-Preparatory School, also at Notting Hill, where he found himself kept busy. In sharp contrast to the two days a week at nursery school, he was now having to be up by 7.30 each weekday morning, washed and dressed before eating breakfast and being taken to his new school where he started lessons in earnest. Reading and writing, the first steps in maths, singing lessons and competitive sport were all on the timetable. After-school activities included piano and swimming lessons, often with Diana. Those formative years with loving parents and caring nannies stood William in good stead for his later life.

An early lesson that every member of the Royal Family has to learn is that they are constantly in the public eye. One of Prince William's first public engagements took place when he was just eight years old, when he accompanied his parents to a visit to Llandaff Cathedral to celebrate St David's Day. With a daffodil in his buttonhole, a visit to the principality from which William takes his title was an appropriate baptism into public life.

Below left: Watched by his cousin Laura Fellowes, a mischievous Prince William, aged three, is caught on camera during the wedding of Prince Andrew and Sarah Ferguson at Westminster Abbey in 1986.

Below right: The shape of things to come: William, watched by Prince Andrew, tries out the controls of his uncle's helicopter on board HMS *Brazen* in 1986.

Above: Prince William entertains and steals the show at his brother Harry's christening in December 1984.

Left: The Prince and Princess of Wales with sons Prince William, right, and Prince Harry prepare for a cycling trip in Tresco during a holiday in the Scilly Isles in 1989.

Prince Harry

Henry Charles Albert David was born on 15 September 1984, like his elder brother William, in the private Lindo Wing of St Mary's Hospital, Paddington. The new baby, known affectionately as 'Harry', was calm and placid and, in his first few years, was a quieter child than William. As with their first child, Prince Charles had stayed by Princess Diana's side during her nine-hour labour and was delighted to have another son. The following morning William, escorted by nanny Barbara Barnes, met his brother for the first time. Later that day the crowds waiting outside the hospital had their first glimpse of Harry, wrapped in a blanket in his mother's arms as she and Charles made their way home to Kensington Palace.

Below: Prince Harry arrives at his nursery school in Notting Hill dressed as a pixie in preparation for the Christmas play in 1987.

The whole family was thrilled with the new arrival, including William who reportedly enjoyed climbing in and out of his brother's cot. Prince Charles delighted in the differences between his sons, including the fact that Harry's long, slender fingers were unlike 'the sausage ones William inherited from me'. As Harry grew, the brothers became playmates and good friends. Their down-to-earth nannies gave the youngsters a steady routine. William and Harry were, in nanny Olga Powell's words, 'just like any other children'. 'Their upbringing was very normal and their parents wanted them to have as ordinary a childhood as they could,' she told journalists. 'If they saw a muddy puddle, they wanted to jump in it and if there was something to climb, they wanted to climb it.'

Despite hours apart when William started school, there was still time for the two brothers to play together, donning Superman outfits or army gear for a game of soldiers, and time for fun at weekends when life went at a more leisurely pace. Whenever possible the family travelled to Highgrove, their country home in Gloucestershire, where they boys had farmland to explore, fields to run round. Their pony, Smokey, would be saddled up for early riding lessons. Prince Harry, just two-and-a-quarter years younger than William, followed his brother to nursery and pre-prep schools. In 1992 he joined William at Ludgrove School in Berkshire,

where they were both pupils until William left for Eton in September 1995, followed by Harry in 1998.

During their marriage, the Prince and Princess of Wales made many overseas visits, which included taking their sons on several occasions. William and Harry were kept out of the limelight as much as possible while their parents carried out their many engagements.

Life for both boys was varied – their mother, wanting them to experience ordinary life, took them to theme parks, burger restaurants and even to night shelters for the homeless so that they could understand other people's lives. Both William and Harry love sport and something they both enjoyed were visits, with Diana, to rugby matches. At Highgrove the love of the countryside the boys shared with Prince Charles saw them enjoying the outdoor life, including spending time on the river where they would learn the rudiments of fishing.

However, being royal could not protect the princes from the upset of the divorce of their parents in 1996, nor from the tragic death of their mother in a car accident the following year, when Harry was not yet 13, and William 15.

Above: The Princess of Wales follows her sons, five-year-old, Prince Harry (right), and Prince William, seven, on Harry's first day at the Wetherby School in Notting Hill, West London in 1989.

Right: Harry looks to his big brother as the siblings are photographed on Harry's first day at Wetherby School.

Princesses Beatrice
& Eugenie

Below left: The Duke and Duchess of York with Princess Beatrice, just two weeks old.

Below right: The Duchess of York gives her daughter Eugenie a kiss after the child's christening at Sandringham in 1990. Cousins Zara Phillips and Prince Harry also join the christening party, and the baby's big sister Princess Beatrice can just be seen at the bottom of the photograph.

The birth of the first child of Prince Andrew and Sarah Ferguson, the Duke and Duchess of York, was eagerly anticipated in August 1988. The baby would be The Queen's fifth grandchild, and the royal mother of four showed her own impatience about the baby's arrival; during a royal visit, asked when it was due, she said: 'These wretched babies don't come until they're ready. They don't come to order.'

A clue that the birth was imminent was the return home, from Singapore where he was serving as a Royal Navy pilot, of Prince Andrew, who drove his wife to London's Portland Hospital on the morning of 8 August. He went with her to her room on the third floor and was beside her during a short labour. The baby girl, unnamed for some days, but dubbed 'Baby Yorklet' by her fond parents, was born in the early evening, weighing 6lb 12oz. 'The baby is very pretty,' Andrew told reporters, 'But then I am very biased.'

By the time he arrived at the end of the week to pick up his wife and his red-haired daughter, then fifth in line to the throne, those waiting outside the hospital had enjoyed witnessing the arrival of Princess Diana and her two sons, the new baby's first cousins, William and Harry (the latter mischievously sticking his tongue out at photographers) and other royal visitors. On leaving hospital, Sarah wore a teddy-bear shaped badge stating 'I'm a mum'. The family of three, in their blue Jaguar, drove to a waiting aircraft that delivered them safely to Scotland, where they were to stay with The Queen at Balmoral and ask her approval for the new baby's name.

The child was christened Princess Beatrice Elizabeth Mary at the Chapel Royal at St James's Palace on 20 December.

A new nanny, Alison Wardley, was engaged to look after Beatrice, who moved with her parents back to the family home, the seven-bedroomed Castlewood House in Surrey, where they were living until the much larger Sunninghill Park mansion in Windsor Great Park was completed. In fact, the new twelve-bedroomed house was still not ready by the time the Duchess went into labour with her second child, less than two years later.

The birth of Princess Eugenie, on 23 March 1990, proved difficult as the unborn child was in a breech position, necessitating an unexpected Caesarean section. But when the Duchess of York checked out of the Portland Hospital a week later, the 7lb 1oz infant was already named Eugenie Victoria Helena, after Queen Victoria's favourite granddaughter, Victoria Eugenie.

Nanny Alison Wardley now had her hands full with the two little girls, but she and they had a new home to move to just six months after Eugenie's birth. Sunninghill Park, with its cinema, swimming pool, tennis courts and children's nursery, was at last ready. Beatrice, now two, had a bedroom painted pink and lemon, while baby Eugenie's night nursery was a pretty lemon and blue.

The Yorks broke with royal tradition when it was Eugenie's turn to be christened. She was baptised in public during a regular Sunday morning service at St Mary Magdalene Church at Sandringham on 23 December, two days before Christmas Day, 1990.

Above: Princes William and Harry with their cousins Princesses Eugenie and Beatrice on a skiing holiday to Klosters in Switzerland in 1995.

Lady Louise Windsor
& James, Viscount Severn

Prince Edward's daughter's entry into the world was both dramatic and traumatic. Lady Louise Windsor, born after her mother, Sophie, Countess of Wessex, had previously suffered an ectopic pregnancy, arrived four weeks early. The Countess was rushed to Frimley Park Hospital in Surrey on 8 November 2003 and had to undergo an emergency Caesarean operation, during which her life was endangered by blood loss. Little Louise, weighing just 4lb 9oz at birth, was taken immediately to the specialist neo-natal unit at St George's Hospital in south London as a precautionary measure, where she stayed for five days, before being sent back to Frimley Park.

Her father, Prince Edward, Earl of Wessex, The Queen's youngest son, was away on royal duty, on a state visit to Mauritius, when his daughter was born, but he flew back immediately to be with his wife and baby. Once it was known that both mother and baby were out of danger, the Countess, who clearly intended to be a hands-on mother, spent as much time with her new daughter as possible, friends reporting that the infant, whose full name is Louise Alice Elizabeth Mary Mountbatten-Windsor, was a 'real cutie-pie' and 'a perfect jolly little baby'.

Louise began to thrive and was discharged from hospital on 23 November, four days after her mother. In December she was taken to join the rest of the Royal Family for the

Right: Prince Edward, Earl of Wessex, carries his toddler daughter, Lady Louise Windsor, on to dry land after a Royal Family boating holiday in the Hebrides in 2006.

traditional Christmas celebrations at Sandringham in Norfolk. It soon became evident that she was doted on not only by her parents, but also by her paternal grandmother, The Queen, who spent more time than usual fussing over the latest addition to the family.

The birth in 2007 of Louise's brother, James Alexander Philip Theo Mountbatten-Windsor, also at Frimley Park Hospital, was far less difficult. Prince Edward was with his wife in a private suite at the hospital as his son was delivered, by Caesarean section, by royal gynaecologist Maurice Setchell on 17 December. The Prince, clearly relieved, told well-wishers and journalists outside the hospital that his baby son was 'small, cute and cuddly'. He added that the baby's arrival was 'a lot calmer than last time, I'm glad to say'.

The Earl and Countess of Wessex live at Bagshot Park, near Windsor Castle, where their children often go to see their grandmother, who likes to spend time with them. Like their grandmother, Louise and James are both passionate about horses and keep their ponies stabled in the Royal Mews at the castle, often riding out with The Queen. Although their grandmother wears her traditional headscarf, she insists that the children wear hard hats.

The Earl and Countess of Wessex are protective of their children and try to keep them out of the limelight, especially Louise who was born with a rare eye condition, exotropia, that affected her sight. Despite this she is an avid reader, and is keen on ballet as well as riding.

Like their cousins Peter and Zara Phillips, neither Louise nor James has taken the title of Prince or Princess as is usual for grandchildren of a reigning monarch. As the daughter of an earl, Louise becomes 'Lady' while James is known by one of his father's titles, Viscount Severn.

Above: Sophie, Countess of Wessex, smiles as she and her husband, Prince Edward, leave hospital with their baby son, James, Viscount Severn.

The Next Generation

The Queen's first great-grandchild, born on 29 December 2010 to her eldest grandson, Peter Phillips, and his Canadian wife, Autumn, made history. The baby – 12th in line to the throne at the time of her birth – had dual Canadian and British citizenship, making her the first Canadian in the British line of succession.

The child's name was made public at a church service on 2 January 2011 at The Queen's Sandringham Estate in Norfolk, attended by the Royal Family, when the Reverend Jonathan Riviere made mention of it in a prayer for 'Peter and Autumn Phillips and their daughter Savannah'. Although the name caused a few eyebrows to be raised in Britain, it is in common use across the Atlantic and has become increasingly popular. Peter Phillips – at the request of his parents, and because Princess Anne holds no hereditary title – has no royal title, and his daughter follows suit.

Peter met Autumn Kelly in 2003 at the Montreal Grand Prix, where they were both working. They became engaged in 2007 and were married at St George's Chapel, Windsor in May 2008. Autumn Phillips, a former Roman Catholic, was accepted into the Church of England shortly before their wedding, because the 1701 Act of Settlement decreed that her husband would have had to give up his right to the throne had she not done so; the Act changed in 2013.

After living in Hong Kong, where Peter Phillips was working, the couple moved back to London soon before Savannah Anne Kathleen, weighing 8lb 8oz, was born at the Gloucestershire Royal Hospital near Gatcombe Park, the home of her grandmother, Princess Anne. The Queen, 'delighted' at the arrival of the latest addition to the Royal Family, became the first reigning monarch to have a great-grandchild since Queen Victoria more than 100 years before.

Above left: Savannah (left) and Isla Phillips (right) play with their cousin Mia Tindall before watching Zara Tindall compete at Badminton Horse Trials, May 2016.

Below left: The Duke of Cambridge takes Prince George and Princess Charlotte to visit their new brother at St Mary's Hospital in London in April 2018.

Prince George's birth meant that for the first time since Queen Victoria's reign – when her great-grandson, the future Edward VIII, was born in 1894 – the monarchy has three generations of heirs to the throne. In 1894 they were Queen Victoria's son Bertie, later Edward VII, his son, who became George V, and the ill-fated Edward VIII, who abdicated in 1936. Now the heirs are Prince Charles, Prince William and Prince George.

Savannah was christened at Holy Cross Church, Avening, Gloucestershire in February and the following month made her first public outing at the annual horse trials at Gatcombe Park. Her sister, Isla Elizabeth Phillips, was born on 29 March 2012, also at Gloucestershire Royal Hospital, weighing 7lb 4oz. It was thought to be no coincidence that her second name was the same as that of her great-grandmother who was celebrating her Diamond Jubilee that year.

A year later, 8 July 2013, came the announcement that Zara (née Phillips) and her husband, former rugby player Mike Tindall – who was a member of the 2003 World Cup-winning squad – were expecting their first child. Just days later, The Queen's third great-grandchild was born: Prince George, son of the Duke and Duchess of Cambridge.

Zara and Mike were engaged in December 2010 and married the following summer at Canongate Kirk in Edinburgh. Since 2013 the couple have lived on the Gatcombe Park Estate, as do Peter Phillips and his family. Mia Grace Tindall was born on 17 January 2014, delivered, like her cousins Savannah and Isla, at Gloucestershire Royal Hospital. Mia's christening took place on 30 November that year, at St Nicholas' Church, Cherington – the same Gloucestershire church where Isla Phillips was baptised on 1 July 2012.

On the occasion of The Queen's 90th birthday in 2016, an official portrait was taken of Her Majesty with her two youngest grandchildren – twelve-year-old Lady Louise and eight-year-old Viscount Severn – and all five of her great-grandchildren. But it was two-year-old Mia who stole the show when she hoisted aloft her great-grandmother's handbag. Sitting on The Queen's lap for the photograph was the youngest member of the family, William and Catherine's second-born child, eleven-month-old Princess Charlotte.

Above: Pageboy Prince George (second right) and flower girl Princess Charlotte (far left) leave St Mark's Church, Englefield Green following the marriage of their aunt Pippa Middleton to James Matthews in May 2017.

Prince George

The Duke and Duchess of Cambridge had been married just over 18 months when, on 30 November 2012, Catherine visited her old school, St Andrew's in Pangbourne, Berkshire, where, despite wearing high heels, she showed her prowess on the hockey pitch; who would have guessed that three days later would come the news that she was pregnant? The announcement was made before the customary 12 weeks in view of the Duchess being admitted to hospital, suffering from debilitating morning sickness. When the pregnancy was announced, Prime Minister David Cameron spoke for the nation when he said, 'It's absolutely wonderful news and I'm sure everyone around the country will be celebrating with them tonight.'

On 22 July 2013, the hottest day of the year, George Alexander Louis, the Prince of Cambridge, was born at St Mary's Hospital, Paddington, weighing 8lbs 6oz. Although the birth took place at 4.24 p.m., it was not until 8.30 p.m. that the official announcement came, his parents wanting to share those first precious hours alone with their baby. Breaking with royal tradition, an official notification of the birth was given to the press via email from Kensington Palace before the customary framed announcement was fixed to an ornate easel on the forecourt of Buckingham Palace. Clarence House also tweeted the details on Twitter.

The royal birth was marked by two gun salutes, at Green Park and the Tower of London, while the bells of Westminster Abbey rang out in celebratory peal for three hours. There was a heartfelt message from the baby's royal grandfather, Prince Charles, who said, 'Both my wife and I are overjoyed at the arrival of my first grandchild. Grandparenthood is a unique moment in anyone's life, as countless kind people have told me in recent months, so I am enormously proud and happy to be a grandfather for the first time.'

Below left: Prince George in his mother's arms as they arrive in Wellington for the first day of the Duke and Duchess of Cambridge's tour of New Zealand, April 2014.

Below right: Prince William and Princess Charlotte look on as Prince George plays with a bubble gun at a children's party at Government House in Victoria, British Columbia, in 2016.

William and Catherine spent that first night in hospital with their son before introducing him to the world and a barrage of flashing cameras the next day. Like his father and grandfather before him, this was no ordinary baby, but a child born to one day be king – though just then the new Prince slept on, unaware of the weight of history on his tiny shoulders. The Queen's third great-grandchild, and first great-grandson, will eventually be the 43rd monarch since William the Conqueror, who won the English Crown at the Battle of Hastings in 1066, and the 8th monarch to descend from Queen Victoria.

The family of three made their way home to Kensington Palace that day. From 2015, a second home at Anmer Hall on the Sandringham Estate in Norfolk meant Prince William, at that time a helicopter pilot for East Anglian Air Ambulance, was not separated from his wife and child.

Prince George made his second public appearance at his christening on 23 October 2013. From day one, William and Catherine have been keen to protect him, and subsequently his siblings, from the pressures of public duty, keeping him out of the media spotlight as much as possible and choosing to share official photographs when appropriate. George's next major public appearance, therefore, was highly newsworthy when, in April 2014, he travelled with his parents on an official visit to New Zealand and Australia. Two months later he was seen toddling in public for the first time while attending a charity polo match in Cirencester in which his father and uncle, Prince Harry, were playing.

In January 2016 George started at Westacre Montessori School nursery in Norfolk, near his home at Anmer Hall. Following Prince William's decision to leave the East Anglian Air Ambulance service in summer 2017 to spend more time on royal duties, the family relocated more permanently to Kensington Palace, and in September George became a pupil at Thomas's Battersea prep school in south London, for children aged four to 13. In November 2017, his mother revealed that, like many small children, her son is interested in dinosaurs, which he was learning about at school, and that he especially liked the T-Rex because it was 'the noisiest and scariest'.

Above: Prince George, prepared for his first day at Thomas's Battersea school in September 2017.

Six months prior to Prince George's birth, The Queen overturned a 1917 decree that meant if William and Catherine's first child had been a daughter she would have been known as Lady, rather than Her Royal Highness. A Letters Patent issued by King George V had limited titles within the Royal Family, meaning that only a first-born son of the Prince of Wales' eldest son was automatically entitled to be styled a prince. However, the new declaration states that 'all the children of the eldest son of the Prince of Wales should have and enjoy the style, title and attribute of royal highness with the titular dignity of Prince or Princess prefixed to their Christian names or with such other titles of honour'.

Princess Charlotte

On Saturday 2 May 2015 came the news that the second child of the Duke and Duchess of Cambridge had arrived safely at 8.34 a.m., weighing 8lb 3oz. As many had hoped, including expectant grandfather Prince Charles, the baby was a girl. London welcomed the child with the iconic BT Tower scrolling 'It's a girl' and, as night fell, other landmarks, including Tower Bridge and the fountain in Trafalgar Square, were glowing pink.

Just 12 hours after arriving at St Mary's Hospital, Paddington, the baby's parents emerged with their daughter, their smiles telling the world how happy they were. Happy, too, were their families. The Queen, dressed in pink and attending an official engagement at Richmond in North Yorkshire, beamed when congratulated on her newest great-granddaughter. Prince Charles and the Duchess of Cornwall reported that they were 'absolutely delighted'.

The baby's names were announced two days later: Charlotte Elizabeth Diana. The new family of four first appeared together in public as they arrived for Charlotte's christening at Sandringham on 5 July – the baby comfortable in the pram previously used for her uncles, Princes Andrew and Edward – for the ceremony conducted by the Archbishop of Canterbury, Justin Welby.

Charlotte became the first baby to take the title Princess of Cambridge since George III's granddaughter, born in 1833. She is the most senior princess born since Princess Anne in 1950. There had not been a new princess in the Royal Family for 25 years, since the birth of Princess Eugenie, youngest daughter of the Duke and Duchess of York.

There was great media interest when, in September 2016, Charlotte made her first overseas trip, travelling with her parents and brother on an official visit to Canada. In July 2017 the children joined their parents on an official visit to Poland and Germany. In January 2018, the Princess – described by her father as having a 'sweet nature' and by her mother as 'extremely chatty' – posed on the steps of Kensington Palace as she prepared for her first day at Willcocks Nursery School in Kensington: a big day for any child and no less so for the little girl who is fourth in line to the royal throne.

Top: Just a few hours after she was born, and cosy in a woollen shawl and bonnet against a chill spring wind, Princess Charlotte was introduced to the waiting press as she left hospital.

Middle: The Princess in her Silver Cross pram as she leaves her christening at the Church of St Mary Magdalene in Sandringham, Norfolk in July 2015.

Bottom: Pretty as a picture: Princess Charlotte in Berlin during a three-day tour of Germany with her parents and Prince George in July 2017.

Prince Louis

A statement released by Kensington Palace in September 2017 announced that the Duchess of Cambridge was expecting her third child, and on St George's Day 2018 the world welcomed the news that she had been delivered of a son, a son weighing 8lb 7oz.

The safe arrival of the little boy at 11.01 a.m. on 23 April was announced shortly after 1 p.m., just a few hours after the Duchess had been whisked into St Mary's Hospital. The newest family member was the heaviest of William and Catherine's children, topping older brother George by just one ounce.

The child, who is fifth in line to the throne, made his first public appearance seven hours after his birth when his parents greeted the crowds outside the hospital before driving home to Kensington Palace. The Duchess, elegant in a red dress with white lace collar – the colours of the flag of St George – cradled her son in her arms; the Duke held up three fingers and joked that he now had 'thrice the worry'. Earlier he had taken Prince George and Princess Charlotte to visit their new brother. George looked somewhat serious, but his sister was happy to wave for the cameras.

Four days after his birth, the names of the new Prince were confirmed as Louis Arthur Charles, the choice of first name honouring Lord Mountbatten, an important figure in the lives of both Prince Philip and Prince Charles.

Prince Louis's arrival was perfect timing, giving four weeks for the excitement to subside before the next major royal event: the marriage of Prince Harry to Meghan Markle on 19 May.

Far right: The Duchess of Cambridge with her newborn son outside the Lindo Wing at St Mary's Hospital in Paddington, London.

Right: A notice is placed on an easel in the forecourt of Buckingham Palace to formally announce the birth of a baby boy to the Duke and Duchess of Cambridge on 23 April 2018.

The birth of the Duke and Duchess of Cambridge's third child in 2018 brought the number of great-grandchildren with which Queen Elizabeth II was blessed at that time to six. But, remarkably, Queen Victoria had 85 great-grandchildren, the last of whom, Count Carl Johan Bernadotte, died in 2012. The fifth child of the King of Sweden, Prince Carl Johan renounced his royal title in 1946 when he married divorcee and commoner Elin Kerstin Margaretha Wijkmark.

Royal Christenings

Soon after the birth of Princess Elizabeth in 1926, the chairman of the National Jewellers' Association arrived at the family home in Bruton Street. He carried an exquisitely wrapped present for the baby, made by members of his organisation. The beautiful silver porringer, a little bowl with ivory handles carved to resemble thistles and a cover decorated with an ivory and silver coronet, would, he hoped, be placed 'upon the breakfast table of the first baby in the land'.

The baby received other silver gifts from her godparents (or 'sponsors' as royal godparents are known) at her christening in the private chapel at Buckingham Palace at the end of May. Although the ceremony was a family occasion, there were present ten 'Children of the Chapel Royal', choirboys with unbroken voices who wore crimson and gold uniform with old-lace jabots, bringing colour and traditional music to the ceremony. The service was conducted by the then Archbishop of York, Cosmo Lang.

The little Princess was carried into the chapel by her nanny, Clara Knight. She came to the rescue when the sobbing baby, dressed in the fine Honiton lace and silk christening robe, refused to be comforted, as the family gathered around the ornate font. Alla, who had come prepared, dosed her tiny charge with several spoonfuls of traditional old-fashioned dill water. The small party of close family and friends made their way back to Bruton Street for a tea party, the centrepiece of which was an elegant cake, decorated with the white roses of York surrounding a small silver cradle, and cut by the Duchess of York.

Elizabeth's sister, Princess Margaret Rose, was also christened by Archbishop Cosmo Lang in 1930. The venue for the ceremony was the chapel at Buckingham Palace. Margaret's christening cake, made in Scotland, was so large that there was enough to send each household in the village of Glamis, near her mother's family home, a slice.

Gifts, whether to celebrate the birth or the christening, are showered upon royal babies. When the baby who became Queen Elizabeth I was christened at three days old in 1533, her gifts included a 'standing cup of gold' from her godfather Thomas Cranmer, Archbishop of Canterbury. It took 'four noble gentlemen' to carry the gifts presented by her godparents from the church back to the palace at Greenwich. In the years following her namesake Princess Elizabeth's birth in 1926, the baby's parents, the Duke and Duchess of York, embarked without her on a six-month tour of Australia. When they returned it was with three tons of gifts – including several parrots – for their baby daughter. More than 80 years later, when her 21-month-old great-grandson Prince George visited New Zealand and Australia in 2014 his many gifts included a toddler-sized speedboat and miniature surfboard.

Top: Detail of the decoration on Prince Charles' official christening cake, 1948.

Above: When not being used for royal baptisms, the fabulous silver-gilt Lily Font is kept, with other royal treasures, in the Tower of London.

Right: Four generations of monarchs: Queen Victoria holds the baby who would be King Edward VIII, on his christening day, 16 July 1894. The baby, dressed in the beautiful Honiton lace christening gown first worn by his great-aunt Princess Victoria in 1841, is flanked on either side by his grandfather (later Edward VII) and father (later George V).

Royal christenings of the past invariably featured the traditional family Honiton lace christening robe and the beautiful silver-gilt Lily Font, commissioned by Queen Victoria in 1840 and first used for the christening of her daughter, Victoria, in 1841. The water used to baptise the baby is sent from the river Jordan. The ceremony, which lasts about 30 minutes, is conducted by an archbishop, often the Archbishop of Canterbury. The Royal Family, godparents and guests stand near the font, waiting for the baby to be carried into the room by his or her nanny, accompanied by a lady-in-waiting. After the christening ceremony and the singing of hymns or anthems, the baptismal register is signed, before a reception where lunch or tea, depending on the time of day, is served, along with christening cake.

Born to be king: Prince William was christened at Buckingham Palace on 4 august 1982. This christening photograph shows members of the royal family and William's godparents: Sir Laurens Van der Post, Princess Alexandra Duchess of Westminster, ex-King Constantine of Greece, Lady Susan Hussey and Lord Romsey.

Three of the children of The Queen and Prince Philip were baptised in the Buckingham Palace Music Room, an imposing chamber with a high-domed ceiling, arched windows and columns painted deep blue to look like lapis lazuli. Prince Charles, Princess Anne and Prince Andrew, all wearing the family christening gown, were welcomed to the fellowship of the Church, surrounded by their godparents, or sponsors.

Prince Edward was the exception, being christened in the private Chapel at Windsor Castle on 2 May 1964 by the then Dean of Windsor, Robert Woods. Charles and Andrew were christened by the Archbishop of Canterbury, Dr Geoffrey Fisher, while Dr Cyril Garbett, Archbishop of York, officiated at Princess Anne's baptism. Prince Andrew's nurse, June Waller, reported that her young charge behaved very well at his baptism – not crying 'except for two little squeaks'.

Princes William and Harry were both christened by the then Archbishop of Canterbury, Robert Runcie, but, while William's ceremony took place, as had his father's, in the Buckingham Palace Music Room, Harry was baptised at St George's Chapel, Windsor.

There was a break with the recent tradition of future monarchs being christened at Buckingham Palace when the ceremony for Prince George took place at the Chapel Royal at St James's Palace, conducted by the Archbishop of Canterbury, Justin Welby. It was an intimate affair with just 22 guests, mainly senior royals, immediate members of the Middleton family and godparents. After the ceremony, a private tea party in the baby's honour was held at Clarence House, hosted by the Prince of Wales and Duchess of Cornwall.

It was all change again when Princess Charlotte was christened at St Mary Magdalene Church on the Sandringham Estate where the Royal Family worship – most famously on Christmas morning – when they are in residence. It was at this church that William's mother, Diana, Princess of Wales, was christened in 1961.

Christening cakes for royal babies are always splendid confections but little Prince Charles, christened in December 1948, had not one, but three, all on display during the family reception in the White Drawing Room at Buckingham Palace after the religious ceremony. The first was a redecorated version of the top tier of his parents' wedding cake, made glorious with intricate 'lace' icing topped with a baby doll sleeping in a silver cradle and dressed in a magnificent robe, sewn by members of the Royal School of Art Needlework. The second was an enormous coronet-topped, three-foot (one-metre) high cake, made by students from the National School of Bakery with ingredients contributed from countries of the British Empire. The third cake, of two tiers, given by the Universal Cookery and Food Association, was decorated with silver ornaments made by disabled silversmiths. Both Prince William's and Prince George's christening cakes were also redecorated versions of a tier of their parents' wedding cakes.

All of The Queen's children and grandchildren had splendid christening presents, one of the most magnificent being the antique silver-gilt cup, given to Prince Charles in 1948 by his great-grandmother and godparent, Queen Mary. The beautiful object was made by English silversmith Thomas Heming in 1773 for King George III, who had given it as a christening gift to the son of a friend.

Top right: The precious silk and lace 16th-century christening robe, thought to have been made for Princess Elizabeth (later Queen Elizabeth I) in 1533.

Bottom right: The Duchess of Cambridge carries Prince George as they arrive for his christening in October 2013. The baby is wearing the christening gown commissioned in 2008 by his great-grandmother, Queen Elizabeth II, and first worn by James, Viscount Severn.

Far right: The Queen Mother, holding Prince William, laughs with Prince Charles and The Queen at Prince William's christening in August 1982.

The Honiton lace gown had been worn by royal babies at their christenings for 167 years and was beginning to look a little tired when The Queen decided to commission a hand-made replica from royal dressmaker Angela Kelly. The beautiful copy of the original gown was ready in time for the baptism, in April 2008, of baby James, Viscount Severn, the infant son of the Earl and Countess of Wessex.

Royal Succession

Succession to the throne in the 21st century is not such a contentious issue as in the days when battles were fought to claim the Crown and reigning monarchs were killed or had to flee into exile.

In 1066 William, Duke of Normandy, seized his chance when Edward the Confessor died with no heir. William, emerging victorious over Harold Godwinson, who had reigned for just a few months, established a dynasty that ended in civil war as rival factions supported two claimants to the throne: Stephen (who reigned until 1154) and Matilda, daughter of Henry I. Matilda's son, Henry II, eventually succeeded, the first in a long line of Plantagenets whose rule ended with the death of Richard III, defeated at the Battle of Bosworth in 1485 by Henry Tudor, who became King Henry VII.

Richard allegedly destroyed potential Plantagenet successors by killing Henry VI, his own brother, George, and his two young nephews – the uncrowned Edward V and his brother, Richard, Duke of York – who disappeared in suspicious circumstances.

Fears over the succession were raised again with the death of the childless 'Virgin Queen', Elizabeth I. The Crown went to James VI of Scotland, son of Mary, Queen of Scots, who had been executed in 1587 on Elizabeth's orders. James became James I of England and was succeeded by his son, Charles, who upset Parliament so much that civil war erupted and all thought of succession ceased as Charles was executed in 1649, and the monarchy suspended. But the interregnum ended with the recall from exile of the dead King's son, Charles II, in 1660.

The next upset was in 1685 when Charles II died, to be succeeded by his brother, James II, whose Catholic policies impelled his overthrow

Left: The reigning monarch: Her Majesty Queen Elizabeth II.

Above: Prince Charles, the Prince of Wales and Duke of Cornwall, is first in line to the throne.

It was the forced 'abdication' of James II in 1688, leading to the invitation to his daughter Mary and her husband William, rather than James' young son, to rule that led to the 1689 Bill of Rights and the 1701 Act of Settlement, determining the basis for the succession, not only by descent, but also by Parliamentary statute. These acts established that the Sovereign rules through Parliament, which can regulate the succession to the throne. If the Sovereign is deemed to have misgoverned (as in the case of James II), he or she may be deprived of the title.

Changes were made to rules for the succession in 2013. The previous acts specifically excluded Roman Catholics from the throne and banned the marriage of a sovereign to a Roman Catholic. Now the spouse of a reigning monarch may be a Roman Catholic. The Succession to the Crown Act 2013 also decreed that females born in the line of succession have exactly the same rights as males. An older sister, born after 28 October 2011, no longer has to step aside in favour of a younger brother.

in favour of his (Protestant) daughter Mary and her husband William of Orange, who ruled jointly from 1689 until Mary's death in 1694, when William III ruled alone until he died in 1702. He was succeeded by his sister-in-law, Anne. On her death the throne went to her second cousin, George of Hanover (George I), a deeply unpopular king who spoke not a word of English.

The succession ran more or less smoothly until the abdication of Edward VIII in 1936, when The Queen's father became King. With the accession of Queen Elizabeth II in 1952, the succession became secure. She is the mother of four children, grandmother to eight and a great-grandmother several times over. In 2013, laws changed to allow equal succession rights to males and females – so had William and Catherine's eldest child been a girl, she would have been third in line to the British throne.

The Duke and Duchess of Cambridge's first-born, however, was Prince George. His birth, and that of his siblings, has brought great joy to the Royal Family. With Prince George's grandfather and father in line to take the throne ahead of him, our nation's monarchy is secure for generations to come.

Above: Prince William, Duke of Cambridge, will one day succeed his father, Prince Charles.

Above: Third in the royal line of succession: Prince George of Cambridge.

DIEU·ET·MON·DROIT

GEORGE V = **Princess VICTORIA MARY**
1910–1936   of Teck (d. 1953)
(became first sovereign of   (H.M. Queen Mary)
the House of Windsor 1917)   granddaughter of Adolphus,
                    Duke of Cambridge

EDWARD VIII = **Mrs BESSIE**   **GEORGE VI** = **Lady ELIZABETH BOWES-LYON**   **H.R.H. Prince HENRY** = **Lady ALICE**
Jan–Dec 1936   WALLIS WARFIELD   1936–1952   (H.M. Queen Elizabeth, the Queen   Duke of Gloucester K.G.   MONTAGU-DOUGLAS-SCOT
Duke of Windsor K.G.   (m. 1937, d. 1986)   (b. 1895, d. 1952)   Mother) daughter of Claude,   (b. 1900, d. 1974)   daughter of John Charles, 7
(b. 1894, d. 1972)   14th Earl of Strathmore K.G.   Duke of Buccleuch
                    (b. 1900, m. 1923, d. 2002)   (m. 1935, d. 2004)

H.M. Queen ELIZABETH II = **H.R.H. Prince PHILIP**   **H.R.H. Prince WILLIAM** of   **H.R.H. Prince RICHARD** = **BIRGITTE VAN DEURS**
(b. 1926, m. 1947)   Duke of Edinburgh K.G.   Gloucester (b. 1941, d. 1972)   Duke of Gloucester   (m. 1972)
Ascended the Throne   (b. 1921, m. 1947)   (b. 1944)
6 Feb 1952

                H.R.H. Princess = **ANTONY ARMSTRONG-JONES**
                MARGARET   1st Earl of Snowdon
                (b. 1930, d. 2002)   (m. 1960, div. 1978, d. 2017)

                ALEXANDER = **CLAIRE**   **Lady** = **GARY LEWIS**   **Lady ROSE** = **GEORGE**
                Earl of Ulster   **BOOTH**   **DAVINA**   (m. 2004)   (b. 1980)   **GILMAN**
                (b. 1974)   (m. 2002)   (b. 1977)   (m. 2008)

            XAN WINDSOR   **Lady COSIMA**   **SENNA**   **TANE MAHUTA**   **LYLA**   **RUFUS**
            Baron Culloden   **WINDSOR** (b. 2010)   (b. 2010)   (b. 2012)   (b. 2010)   (b. 2012)
            (b. 2007)

        DAVID 2nd Earl of Snowdon = **Hon. SERENA STANHOPE**   **Lady SARAH** = **DANIEL CHATTO**
            (b. 1961)   (m. 1993)   (b. 1964)   (m. 1994)

            CHARLES Viscount   **Hon. MARGARITA**   **SAMUEL**   **ARTHUR**
            Linley (b. 1999)   (b. 2002)   (b. 1996)   (b. 1999)

Lady **DIANA SPENCER** = **H.R.H. Prince CHARLES** = 2ndly **CAMILLA**   **MARK PHILLIPS** = **H.R.H. The Princess**
(The Princess of Wales)   **Prince of Wales** K.G.   **PARKER BOWLES**   (m. 1973, div. 1992)   **Royal ANNE** (b. 1950)
daughter of John, 8th Earl   (Heir Apparent)   H.R.H. The Duchess of
Spencer (b. 1961, m. 1981,   (b. 1948)   Cornwall (m. 2005)
div. 1996, d. 1997)

    H.R.H. Prince WILLIAM of = **CATHERINE MIDDLETON**   **H.R.H. Prince HENRY** = **MEGHAN MARKLE**   **PETER** = **AUTUMN KELLY**
    Wales Duke of Cambridge K.G.   Duchess of Cambridge   of Wales Duke of   Duchess of Sussex   (b. 1977)   (m. 2008)
    (b. 1982)   (m. 2011)   Sussex (b. 1984)   (m. 2018)

H.R.H. Prince GEORGE   **HRH Princess CHARLOTTE**   **HRH Prince LOUIS**   **SAVANNAH**   **ISLA**
of Cambridge (b. 2013)   of Cambridge (b. 2015)   of Cambridge (b. 2018)   (b. 2010)   (b. 2012)

The House of Windsor

H.R.H. Prince GEORGE
Duke of Kent K.G.
(b. 1902, d. 1942)
=
H.R.H. Princess MARINA
daughter of Prince Nicholas of
Greece and Denmark
(m. 1934, d. 1968)

H.R.H. Prince JOHN
(b. 1905, d. 1919)

H.R.H. Princess MARY
(Princess Royal)
(b. 1897, d. 1965)
=
HENRY LASCELLES
6th Earl of Harewood K.G.
(m. 1922, d. 1947)

KATHARINE WORSLEY
(m. 1961)
=
H.R.H. Prince EDWARD
Duke of Kent
(b. 1935)

H.R.H. Prince MICHAEL of
Kent* (b. 1942)
=
Baroness MARIE CHRISTINE VON REIBNITZ (Mrs TROUBRIDGE)
(m. 1978)

H.R.H. Princess ALEXANDRA
of Kent (b. 1936)
=
Hon. Sir ANGUS OGILVY
(m. 1963, d. 2004)

Lady HELEN
(b. 1964)
=
TIMOTHY TAYLOR
(m. 1992)

Lord FREDERICK WINDSOR
(b. 1979)
=
SOPHIE WINKLEMAN
(m. 2009)

GABRIELLA WINDSOR
(b. 1981)

JAMES
(b. 1964)
=
JULIA RAWLINSON
(m. 1988)

MARINA
(b. 1966)
=
PAUL MOWATT
(m. 1990, div. 1997)

Lord NICHOLAS WINDSOR*
(b. 1970)
=
PAOLA DOIMI DE LUPIS DE FRANKOPARR
(m. 2006)

2 sons,
2 daughters

2 daughters

1 daughter, 1 son

1 daughter, 1 son

3 sons

GEORGE* Earl
of St Andrews
(b. 1962)
=
SYLVANA TOMASELLI
(m. 1988)

GEORGE LASCELLES 7th
Earl of Harewood
(b. 1923, d. 2011)
=
MARIA DONATA (MARION) STEIN (m. 1949,
div. 1967, d. 2014)
=
2ndly
PATRICIA TUCKWELL
(m. 1967,
d. 2018)

Hon. GERALD LASCELLES
(b. 1924,
d. 1998)
=
ANGELA DOWDING
(m. 1952, div.
1978, d. 2007)
=
2ndly
ELIZABETH COLLINGWOOD
(m. 1978, d. 2006)

1 son, 2 daughters

4 sons

2 sons

2ndly **TIMOTHY LAURENCE**
(m. 1992)

H.R.H. Prince ANDREW Duke of
York (b. 1960)
=
SARAH FERGUSON
Duchess of York
(m. 1986, div. 1996)

H.R.H. Prince EDWARD Earl of
Wessex K.G.
(b. 1964)
=
SOPHIE RHYS-JONES
Countess of
Wessex (m. 1999)

ZARA
(b. 1981)
=
MICHAEL TINDALL
(m. 2011)

H.R.H. Princess BEATRICE of York
(b. 1988)

H.R.H. Princess EUGENIE of York
(b. 1990)

Lady LOUISE MOUNTBATTEN-WINDSOR (b. 2003)

JAMES Viscount
Severn (b. 2007)

MIA
(b. 2014)

* Not in succession to the throne

The Order
of Succession

1. HRH Prince Charles, The Prince of Wales

2. HRH Prince William of Wales, The Duke of Cambridge

3. HRH Prince George of Cambridge

4. HRH Princess Charlotte of Cambridge

5. HRH Prince Louis of Cambridge

6. HRH Prince Henry of Wales, Duke of Sussex

7. HRH Prince Andrew, The Duke of York

8. HRH Princess Beatrice of York

9. HRH Princess Eugenie of York

10. HRH Prince Edward, The Earl of Wessex

11. James, Viscount Severn

12. Lady Louise Mountbatten-Windsor

13. HRH Princess Anne, The Princess Royal

14. Peter Phillips

15. Savannah Phillips

16. Isla Phillips

17. Zara Tindall

18. Mia Tindall

19. David Armstrong-Jones, Earl of Snowdon

20. Charles, Viscount Linley

21. Margarita Armstrong-Jones

22. Lady Sarah Chatto

23. Samuel Chatto

24. Arthur Chatto

25. HRH Prince Richard, The Duke of Gloucester

26. Alexander Windsor, Earl of Ulster

27. Xan Windsor, Lord Culloden

28. Lady Cosima Windsor

29. Lady Davina Lewis

30. Senna Lewis